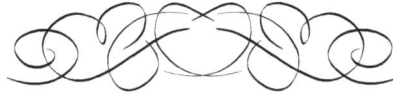

I stand by my decision to put swear words into my son's talker. He was 15, non-verbal, and a high school student. Aidan had been using a talker successfully for a few years by that time, but I controlled what words he could access. I started with the most functional words: EAT, MORE, DRIVE (he uses a wheelchair). Aidan had already shown me that he could use more complex thought patterns to get his point across when he told me HOME BATHROOM SICK GO HOME, and indeed, he had a tummy bug. I was so encouraged by his use of his talker that I didn't even mind when his Uncle Scotty received the first I LOVE YOU.

So we held a family meeting, talked about what swear words were already part of our family culture (that's called modeling), and programmed them into Aidan's talker. And, oh boy did he use them. He used them to try to get out of class one day. His teacher reacted appropriately with him, but she also texted me to share her excitement. Aidan can't talk, but he sure does speak for himself.

Heather

See My ~~Dis~~Abilities

ISBN 13: 978-0-9979317-9-2
ISBN 10: 0-9979317-9-5

Library of Congress PCN 2018944315

Inquiries should be addressed to:

AMITY Publications
www.amitypublications.com

To contact Sue Adler or Debbie Belair or
to order a copy of this book,
please email **tochangethelens@gmail.com**.

Printed in the United States of America

See My D~~is~~Abilities

By Sue Adler and Debbie Belair

A Note from the Authors

We have a professional and personal relationship with the five children featured in this book. We have watched their lives change, seen them grow in ways that never seemed possible.

But remember, the words used to define a disability do not define a person. There are many people with a disability who are waiting for you to discover who they really are.

We invite you to change your lens and "see the abilities." By thinking outside the box and not confining anyone to a "definition", the possibilities are endless.

Sue and Debbie

This book is dedicated to...

all the children and adults who have looked beyond the disability.
Changing our view and "looking through a different lens"
impacts lives in ways we can't imagine.

THANK YOU!

They say I have . . .

Autism Spectrum Disorder (ASD).

Signs of this typically appear during early childhood and affect a person's ability to communicate, and interact with others. ASD is defined by a certain set of behaviors and is a "spectrum disorder" because it affects individuals differently and to varying degrees.

They tell me I may have difficulty . . .

- learning language.
- making eye contact.
- holding a conversation.
- organizing thoughts.
- dealing with noise.
- keeping my body still.
- making new friends.
- showing empathy.
- being an athlete.
- transitioning from one thing to another.
- letting go of a topic.
- being socially comfortable.

But this is who I really am . . .

BAYZIL

JAAGRUTH

They say I have . . .

Down syndrome.

This is a genetic chromosome 21 disorder causing developmental and intellectual delays. There are three types of Down syndrome: Trisomy 21, Translocation, and Mosaicism. Treatment can help, but this condition can't be cured. Down syndrome causes a distinct facial appearance and may be associated with thyroid or heart disease.

They tell me I may have . . .

- poor muscle development.
- heart problems.
- poor judgment.
- slow learning.
- a short attention span.
- impulsive behavior.
- social awkwardness.

But this is who I really am . . .

STELLA

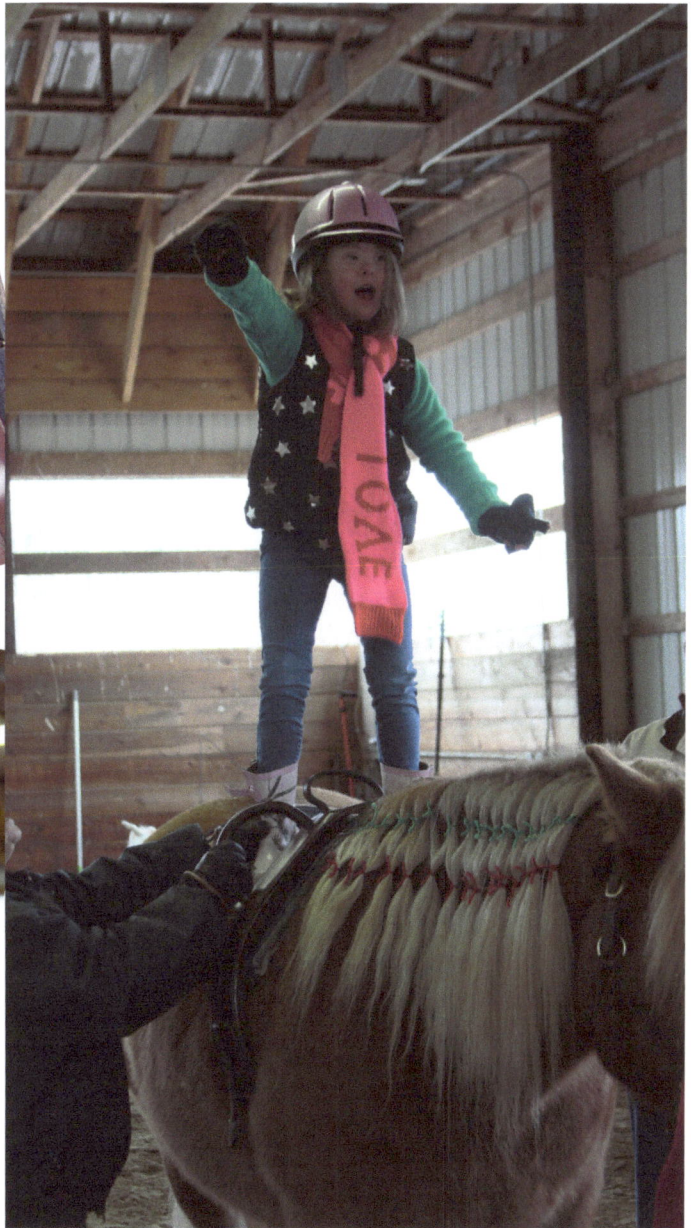

They say I have . . .

PURA syndrome.

This is a rare genetic disorder caused by one of the person's two copies of the PURA gene not functioning normally. Genes are instructions that have important jobs in our growth and development. PURA syndrome can be caused by a "spelling mistake" in those instructions. The PURA gene is known to be particularly important in brain development. When something goes wrong with the PURA gene, it affects the brain which is the boss of the body. So every part of the body can be impacted by this spelling mistake.

They tell me I may have . . .

- difficulty coordinating my body movements.
- cognitive impairments.
- inability to speak.
- seizures.
- no ability to walk without help.
- vision issues.
- feeding difficulties.
- respiratory problems.
- abnormal vision.

But this is who I really am . . .

AIDAN

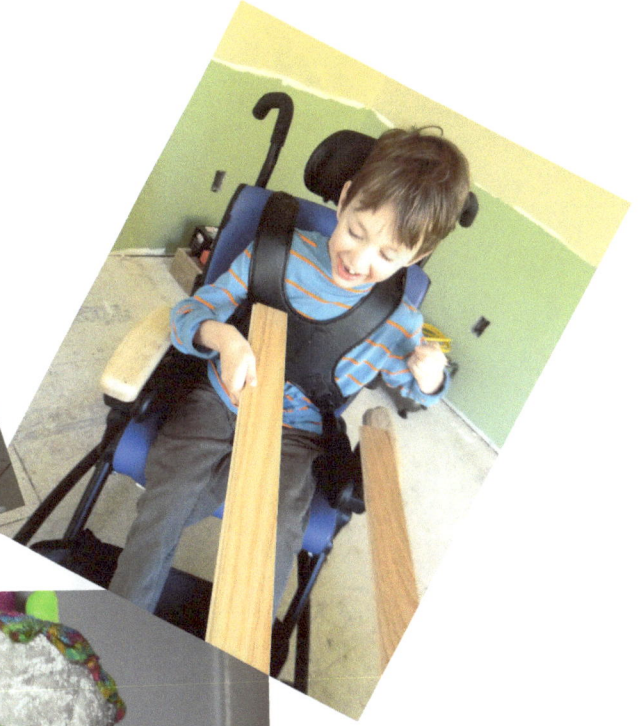

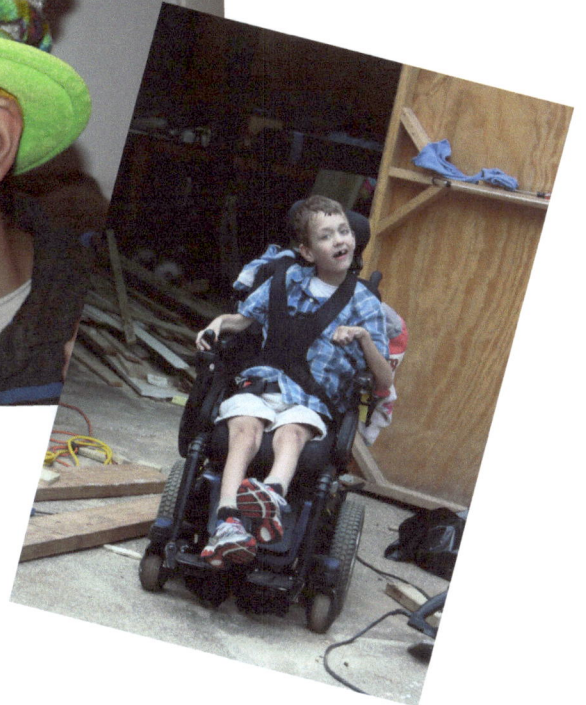

They say I have . . .

DYNC1H1 Gene Mutation.

The DYNC1H1 gene provides instructions for making a protein that is part of a group of proteins called *dynein*. All of our cells need protein to function properly. When something goes wrong with this gene, the instructions do not get to the parts of the body that need it. In other words, the instructions, transported by a train in the body with some broken tracks, do not make it to the final destination. When a muscle or part of the body doesn't have all the instructions it needs, it isn't able to function "normally."

They tell me I may have . . .

- difficulty walking and balancing.
- cognitive impairments.
- an inability to live independently.
- seizures.
- eating issues.

But this is who I really am . . .

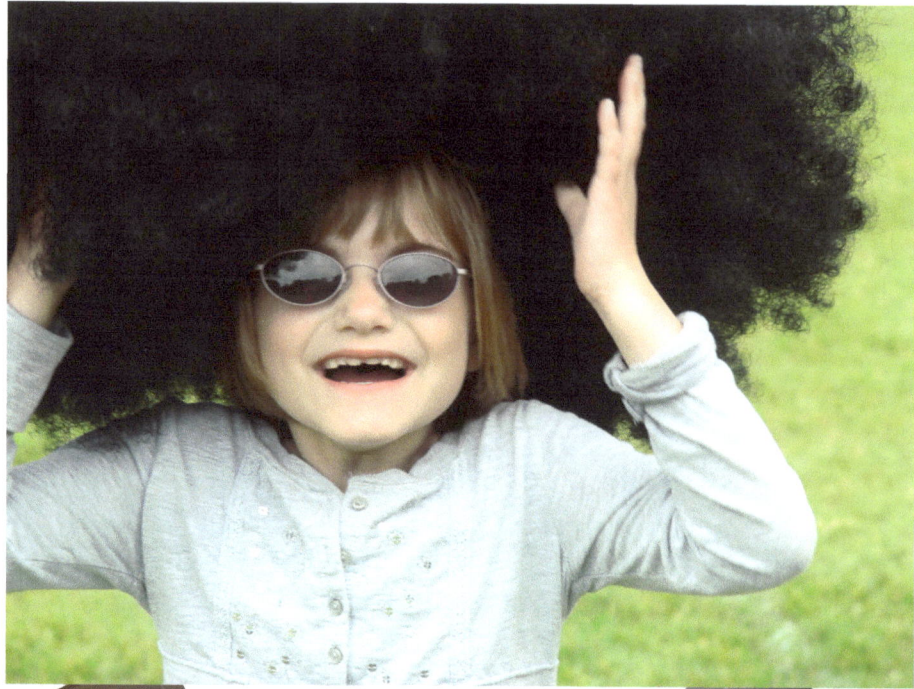

LILY

I remember holding my son, Bayzil, for the first time. He looked so angelic. I stared at this precious, perfect child, and thought to myself, "I will never let anything bad happen to you."

Soon I realized I had/would have very little control over what will inevitably happen to my child, especially when he is out of my immediate grasp. When he was two and a half, it was like a kick in the gut that left me breathless. I heard the litany of things my son would never be able to do because he was given a diagnosis of Autism Spectrum Disorder and Sensory Integration Dysfunction. At that moment, I didn't even know what Autism was. All I knew was that they couldn't possibly be talking about my precious angel. Why wasn't he speaking? Why was he banging his head against a wall, flapping his hands, spinning objects in circles, and starring mesmerized at ceiling fans? Why would he no longer look at me with his loving eyes or when I called his name? It was as if someone had sucked out his soul. He looked off in the distance now with a blank stare.

They say you feel the feelings of your child as they are an extension of you. That could not be a truer statement. Every physical and emotional pain has been felt along the way. On the flip side every triumph and win has been felt through every fiber of my being as well. Watching my son succeed where he was supposed to fail is a sweet victory. There are no words to describe the exhilaration of watching your child, labeled with a disability, soar beyond what you were told they would be capable of by the "experts." He is an angel on Earth, sent to teach so many valuable lessons in life.

Kerri

Jaagurth is so lovable. It doesn't matter if what he is doing is typical or not. He does it immaculately. He is growing and learning fast. We are so proud to tell other parents and care takers how well Jaagurth does things.

We are blessed to have Jaagurth as a child, a member of the family, for who he is, is most important. We are blessed to have a team working with our son, teaching him the life skills he needs to thrive in this fast paced world.

Swapna

We have always been pro-inclusion as far as Stella is concerned. Although we know that activities geared towards people with special needs are wonderful, we also feel very strongly that putting Stella in more challenging environments builds her self-confidence and allows her to push herself.

Stella has been in a typical gymnastics class for the last several months and has just started swim lessons again with a local swim club. She looks to her peers for guidance rather than an adult while trying to master a cartwheel, a forward roll or her back stroke. She waltzes into the gym every week with her frappachino (that she orders herself) and tells me she can go in and change by herself. She is responsible for finding her group and also for her water breaks or bathroom breaks as needed. Swim lessons are much the same. She only moves up to the next level when she has mastered a stroke.

The independence that is required from her gives her self-confidence and respect among her peers. Stella is a huge "cheerleader," yelling words of encouragement and clapping for her friends. She never gets upset for not coming in first or second or third. Although she struggles with independence, she will accomplish it.

Tracey

When Lily was about two years old, we were given the news that she had a moderate brain malformation and her development in all areas would be greatly impacted. It is true that all areas of Lily's development have been impacted but with that comes a great appreciation for all she does, no matter how big or small the milestone.

When she does something that is considered a "typical child's" behavior, it never goes unnoticed and I celebrate her accomplishment. The more you see your child live their life, you realize they will do what they need to do in their own way and time. That is worth celebrating!!!

Nicole

What do YOU see?

www.ingramcontent.com/pod-product-compliance
Lightning Source LLC
LaVergne TN
LVHW070347090426
835511LV00029B/47